JOURNEY INTO LIFE

MISCELLANEOUS WRITINGS OF ERNEST HOLMES • Volume 8

JOURNEY INTO LIFE

ERNEST HOLMES

Compiled and Edited by
WILLIS KINNEAR

SCIENCE OF MIND PUBLICATIONS
Los Angeles, California

Third Printing—January 1980

Published by Science of Mind Publications
3251 West Sixth Street, Los Angeles, California 90020

ISBN: 0-911336-05-2

Printed in the United States of America

Contents

Foreword

In this volume are forty essays – forty days – that can lead to a greater understanding and experiencing of this thing called Life.

They have been carefully selected from the unpublished writings of the late Ernest Holmes – one of the outstanding religious philosophers of our day whose teaching, known as Science of Mind, has beneficially influenced the lives of millions.

In this treasure chest of ideas are vital and dynamic concepts which can add increased joy, happiness, and success to everyone's daily life. They provide a journey that will never be forgotten, for it is inspiring and lifts one to new spiritual heights.

Science of Mind Publications

ACCEPTANCE

We have to accept, just as we accept gravity, that there are self-existent spiritual and mental truths which, when known, will automatically make us free.

We must provide a mold in thought which is equivalent to the thing that we desire. The Law of Mind is a spiritual Power which knows nothing about big and little; It knows nothing about certain persons, but so far as we are concerned, It must always act by reacting to our mental acceptances. That is, It must flow through the channel which we provide, or act in accord with the thought that sets It in motion.

It is the nature of the creative Law of Mind to respond to us, to give us what we ask, when we ask it, and in the way in which we ask it. Thus the childlike mind of acceptance is likened unto the kingdom of heaven. Not faith *in* God, but the faith *of* God is unqualified acceptance.

Our bowl of acceptance must be held up so that it may be filled by the outpouring of Spirit. Its size may be measured in our individual experience according to the law of mental equivalents, which says that whatever we can inwardly conceive, we may outwardly experience. This is because the external is merely a reflection of the internal.

The habit of acceptance should be cultivated and used. Since we automatically attract that which is like our thought, and since our patterns of thought are largely habitual, why not form the habit of expectancy and acceptance?

Our prayers, to be effective, must be affirmations which are so formulated in our mind as to produce an actual inner acceptance of the good desire expressed, even before we have experienced that particular good. We are planting our desire in the garden of a creative Law of Mind which produces a plant exactly like the seed, and never anything else.

ACHIEVEMENT

The creative arts, the accomplishment of any purpose in life, the good that we do to each other, the kindly smile, the peaceful thought, are all some part of that great Divine expression which balances and equalizes and makes sane our everyday life.

The moment a person steps out of the endless stream of humanity he no longer goes by the norm that was set by the mass mind. He is a leader. He is a thinker. He is one who introduces new things into the world. But he has to create the vision ahead of the actual experience.

The Spirit cannot fail. So what we call a failure is merely a limited way in which we are using a limitless Principle that would just as quickly work one way as another. If one has the courage, conviction, and belief to look at a failure and see success, the failure will disappear, resolve itself into a new combination of thought, and a new success will be created.

Every good is ours now, but we must reach out and take this good. The Law of Mind belongs to the man who uses It, and Life belongs to the man who accepts It.

By knowing that every channel for good is open to us we no longer depend upon any one avenue of self-expression, thus limiting the Infinite in Its operation through us to that particular channel.

There is a givingness of the Spirit within us that increases the possibility of our own achievement. When we surrender ourself to the genius of the Universe, the Universe flows into us. Genius is nothing more nor less than the ability of the intellect, will, and emotions to surrender to Something greater than ourself.

The ambition to achieve is the proclamation of our own power to do and to be. The vision we have of a larger experience is but an inner recognition of the infinite potential of the Presence which encompasses all.

APPEARANCES

There is an inner meaning to everything; there is an inside to every fact; there is a hidden cause within every visible effect. This cause is the activity of Spirit.

The Infinite, which is limitless, is also what we call the finite, which appears to be limited, but the finite which appears to be limited is merely the Infinite projecting at the level of the finite.

We live in a world which seems so real, and which is as real as it is supposed to be, but which has no innate reality, no self-determination, no volition or choice.

All effect is subject to its cause. In other words, nothing in our experience projects itself. Our individual world is only a projection of what is first conceived in mind. When the mind withdraws its contemplation from any object, that object begins to disintegrate, whether it is the physical body when the spirit has deserted it, or the body of our affairs when the creative action of mind no longer maintains the pattern for its existence, no longer holds it in the form which creative thought has already given it.

Unless our vision reaches higher, broader, and deeper than the state which we wish to change, how can we hope to change it? We must not become confused by the suggestion of appearance — real as it is, actual as it must be considered to be in human experience. We need to rise above any appearance to that spiritual level of causation above it before we can transform it.

It is not enough to know that God is. We must bring this knowledge into the activity of everyday life. God not only is, but God is in and through every human event. To see this spiritual Presence in things is to look at them in their true nature, to reveal the perfect action of the Presence which dissolves all apparent discord.

BELIEF

We must conclude either that there is an ultimate good and an ultimate evil in the universe, or that there is but one Ultimate which is good, and that this Ultimate, by Its very nature and by our very nature, is compelled to appear to each one of us in the form of our belief.

Simple as it sounds, the world has yet to discover that belief can change anything on earth. The advance of the human race ultimately depends upon its belief in a Power greater than itself and its reaction to the universe in which it lives.

The gift of Life is conditioned in our experience only by our mental receivingness. We receive only what we subjectively accept. A limited belief must produce a limited experience; expanded belief will expand our experiences.

Once we have established a constructive and creative idea for the action of the Law of Mind, no one can remove it but ourselves. There is no person's belief, and no belief of the human race, which can destroy our ideas unless we agree with such belief.

The Spirit goes forth anew into creation through the imagination of any man who dares to believe.

Each of us is acting a role in the great drama of life. Let us stop acting against ourselves, each other, and the world. The imagination can be combined with the will so that each can think of himself as playing a part in the game of life — and a good one. But, in the theater, when a man plays a part that convinces us, he must himself first believe in the part he is playing.

CAUSE AND EFFECT

The Universe holds nothing against us, there is no vindictive God. We cannot destroy the Law but we can and may so alter our position in It that old sequences of cause and effect, which have produced bondage, sickness, trouble, and unhappiness, may instantly become converted into new sequences which will produce opposite results. This is salvation.

Everything in manifestation runs on a time track which is a sequence of a particular chain of cause and effect. But we can erase any such sequence and set in motion a new causation by using the same power of the Law.

The Law of Mind is a law of cause and effect. Thought or idea is the invisible cause; manifestation or the created form is the effect. The form is an outer symbol expressing the idea. Thoughts are acted upon by the Law of Mind which responds with mathematical exactness to the ideas presented to It.

We must always be sure that our word — our prayer — is in harmony with eternal Reality. When we turn our prayer over to the Law we are setting cause and effect in motion. And if we wish to experience only that which is good, our use of the Law must be good. This is but another way of saying that the Universe is foolproof.

Time, space, and conditions are the effects of mental causes through the action of the Law of Mind. Any sequence of cause and effect is relative to the mind which conceives this sequence, and it is equally necessary to understand that the mind which conceives any particular sequence may as easily project another and different one.

The Universe is a combination of spontaneous thought and a mathematical reaction to it. In other words, there is a Divine Presence knowing, and a universal Law responding.

COMMUNION

If we conceive of the Divine Being as separated from us, any communication must be across the void which separates us. Communion with the Infinite is possible only on the supposition that the Infinite is omnipresent, and if omnipresent, at the center of our own being.

The personal aspect of God, the spiritual essence of Reality, is the Divine Intelligence with which we may commune. By intuition, meditation, and prayer we bring ourselves into a conscious and direct relationship with the Spirit within us.

We enter a state of true spiritual communion in such degree as we turn the inner gaze upward, leaving behind the opposite states of doubt, fear, and uncertainty, and dropping all external confusion from our mental attention.

Spirit is the very breath of our life, and because Spirit is All-in-All, and because this Allness is in and through us, when we commune with the deep self we are talking to God. From this Divine communication we receive inspiration, direction, and guidance. We become equipped with an interior awareness which wings our thought, causing it to rise above things as they are, into the contemplation and acceptance of things as they should be right now.

In the mirror of the objective universe we behold the marvelous manifestations of a subtle, invisible Spirit, and as we enter into communion with Its innumerable forms we are, through them, communing with Spirit Itself.

Prayer is our communion with the Spirit, and faith is our definite acceptance that through this communion a Law of Mind reacts to us according to our belief. But someone may ask: Why cannot we have the faith without the communion? The answer is another question: Can an artist paint a beautiful picture unless he communes with beauty?

CONSCIOUSNESS

There must be an infinite Intelligence in the universe which is conscious by reason of the fact that we are conscious. It is impossible to describe the nature of this infinite Consciousness, but we can understand It because we are akin to It.

The self-knowingness of man constitutes his true and only real conscious being and is, as it were, his share of the Cosmic Consciousness, the Mind of God. The difference is not in essence but in degree.

Our awareness of Spirit is not only our awareness of It; it is also Its awareness of us. They are the same thing. Man's consciousness of himself is God's consciousness of man. As man's consciousness expands he becomes more and more God-conscious.

The entire being of man — insofar as we can understand his being — must consist of different states of consciousness. Man lives in his states of consciousness, moves and has his being in them.

The birth of a new state of consciousness is an inner transformation. It is a state of consciousness which no longer depends upon the condition as it appears to be, but which reaches through the seen to the unseen, which plunges beneath the surface and arrives at the spiritual Cause of things.

Do not allow any man to close the door of your thought to that which your spirit instinctively and intuitively senses. There is a realm of consciousness which, while it does not nor can it ever transcend law and order, can and will transcend human experience.

The reason people are poor, miserable, sick, and unhappy is because their consciousness is choked with the weeds of wrong concepts. All the phenomena of life, all the manifestations of living are but experiences revolving around a central atmosphere of consciousness.

CREATION

Creation is the manifestation of an invisible Intelligence, Power, and Law. It is the Creator clothed in definite form. Creation shows selective volition, intelligent direction, and universal diffusion.

God without creation would have no existence. Creation without God would have no reason for being.

Creation is not a finished product but an eternal emanation. All life is an effect, a way, an outward manifestation of interior causes, silently working within themselves and shaping things at last to fit the Divine mandate.

The creative Spirit does not make something out of nothing. Creation means the passing of Spirit into form. It is the play of Life upon Itself.

The infinite variations of life, the eternal manifestations of creation, point to the fact that the Infinite clothes Itself in form in order that It may enjoy Its own Being. It must do this through the power of Its own Imagination, backed by the Law of Its own Word.

In change is the permanent; in the finite is the Infinite; in the form is the Thing giving form, Itself formless but forever taking form.

The descent of Spirit into the world of form does not mean that the Spirit exists in some particular place or sphere of action and then lets Itself be confined, as it were, to that lower plane or sphere of action. It really means the passing of Being into a state of becoming.

The Infinite could not impose limitation on Its creation without limiting Itself, which would be impossible.

The painting of a picture that expresses life and beauty is just as important in the Divine scheme of things as the creation of a cosmos. It takes every man's wholeness to produce the great mosaic of life.

CREATIVITY OF THOUGHT

Man is one with the original Cause of all. This is the reason for the creative power of man's thought. It is not so much a gift of the Spirit as it is the inevitable nature of necessity.

There are not two originators. There is only one. The universal side of man is God; the universal "I Am" is the abstract essence of the individualized "I." Man's thought is creative, not because he wills it to be so, but because it is the will of the Universe, the nature of Being.

There is no question about the creativeness of thought. The only question is, how are we going to use this creative agency within us? Shall we use it consciously and constructively and for definite purposes? Or shall we use it unconsciously and more or less destructively, merely because we do not understand it? The Science of Mind is the answer to this question.

If *any* thought is creative, it must follow that *all* thought is creative. The Law of Mind is exact, not capricious. However, since man's belief is his use of the Law, it must follow that the greater the conviction, the more power his word will have. Therefore, constructive prayer, treatment, or meditation is more powerful than mere idle words.

Thoughts are literally things; they do not operate upon things. The universe in which we live is a system of Intelligence, governed by Law, which operates mechanically, always producing an inevitable result.

Thought creates all the conditions we experience somewhere along the line, but the thinker creates his thoughts.

We are scientific gardeners when we have learned that seedtime and harvest time are independent of any existing circumstances whatsoever. The Garden of God is ever fertile, ever creative, ever productive, and our own thought, will, and imagination scatter the seeds of our planting in Its creative soil. Nothing can hinder the harvest but ourselves.

EXPERIENCE

There is something in us which was never put there by experience, but of which all experience is the outcome.

Thought is the essential activity in the universe. It is the father of all action and the creator of all experience. We all automatically attract to ourselves that which we subjectively embody.

Evolution is an awakening of consciousness to the Essence which is already within us, pushing out for self-expression so that the Infinite may delight Itself in everything that It does, and see in each of us that which It knows Itself to be.

There is a demand made upon every person to be what he really is, or to become what he really is. Becoming is not born out of nothing, but passes from Being into actuality through experience.

Our thought has not projected the universe in which we live, but it has projected our experience in this universe. Our loves, hates, fears, mistakes, hopes, and joys are our mental states which existed before we actually experienced them.

Without consciousness there could be no experience. If we are successful in changing the consciousness, we shall at the same time be successful in changing the experience.

We should affirm nothing that we do not understand, accept nothing that seems irrational, but always keep our minds open to be convinced, never against our will but by the logic of events. We should always reserve the prerogative of choosing what we shall think, but never be unwilling to accept the testimony of what our thought has created in our experience.

FAITH

When faith collides with fact and the two seem contradictory, either we misinterpret the fact or misplace our faith. A fact which is true will never contradict a faith which is true because the Universe is never divided against Itself.

Faith has been the most dynamic power throughout the ages, and it should not be denounced as mere suggestion. But, on the other hand, understanding that faith demonstrates a Principle, we should seek to understand the Principle, and we should make every endeavor to reproduce at will the too infrequent experiences which result from an attitude of faith.

One law of nature does not destroy another. That is why we

may know that fact and faith need never collide; they will operate side by side, but one will be transcendent of the other.

It takes less energy to live constructively than it does destructively. It takes no energy at all to have faith, but fear devastates such energy as we have. It takes no energy to love, it is hate that is destructive. It takes no energy to be happy, but unhappiness and morbidity consume so much energy that we are devitalized mentally and physically. It takes no energy to build up hope, it is despair that blocks us. All it takes is faith.

The veil between Spirit and matter is very thin. The invisible passes into visibility through our faith in it. Out of the liquid of Faith the solid of Fact is formed.

Fear and faith are merely two ways of thinking; each uses the same Power.

The response of the Almighty to our faith must remain commensurate with our faith. This is why it is done unto us as we believe.

FORGIVENESS

Everything that is understood will be forgiven. The past is gone when we learn to forgive and to forget.

The Essence of Spirit lies about us in an unformed state and it is Its nature to take the form of our desires. When these desires are harmonious our lives will flow along with the currents of Cosmic creation; when they are discordant we create confusion for ourselves. But the harmony of Reality always dissipates the confusion of our false thoughts and acts. This is the Divine Forgiveness.

We are all human beings on the pathway of an eternal progress and we all make mistakes. But these mistakes are never held against us and the suffering from them exists only while we indulge in them. The Divine Giver is also the Divine Forgiver.

We have all made many mistakes in this life because of human ignorance. We have all done many things that we ought to have left undone. But unless we can feel that love and forgiveness are eternal we would store up such a sense of condemnation within ourselves that we could not come to the point where we could even forgive ourselves for our own mistakes. And if we could not forgive ourselves, we would always have an unconscious feeling that God, the Divine Giver, does not forgive us.

Is the sun less warm because we stand in the shadow? Is the water less wet because we do not drink, or the glow of the fire less cheerful because we go where it is not? Man will have to learn to forgive himself, but he cannot do it unless he stops doing that which hurts. That is the only thing that the Universe asks of us.

As we listen deeply to That within us which is Divine, we shall find that our accusations against others silently slip away and something seems to say to us, "Neither do I condemn thee."

FREEDOM

Whatever our nature is, we did not create it; we can only use it. As ignorance of the law excuses no one from its effects, and as we are all ignorant of our true natures, we are all bound by this ignorance. This bondage is not an eternal verity, yet it is an actual fact. Enlightenment alone can produce freedom.

The limitation in our lives is the result of ignorance. In reality this apparent limitation is the way we are using our freedom. We shall spring full-orbed into power when we have first grown, consciously, into the real likeness of perfect harmony – perfect harmony with the Divine Presence.

Freedom already exists, like truth and beauty, but it exists in an abstract and formless state. It can only take the form which thought gives it; therefore the thought of limitation creates the very limitation conceived by that thought. Freedom and bondage are merely two ways of expressing a limitless possibility.

Man could not possibly be free unless he had self-choice. Unless his self-choice had the power to bring about at least a temporary manifestation of the thing chosen, he would remain in a dream world, his life would be an hallucination, an illusion, and not a reality.

The world is deluded, blinded, and shackled by its own acceptance of negative thought. It lies bound in chains of its own forging. Mind, which is man's greatest gift, has been made his jailer and he whimpers in a misery entirely of his own creation. Bondage exists nowhere in the universe except in the mind of man. And freedom is his at the precise moment that he recognizes his liberty, and steps forth a free man.

Every limitation we have, every bondage we have, proclaims the freedom which would obtain if we reversed the way we are thinking.

FRIENDSHIP

There is something in the emotional experience of sympathy, of love, and of friendship, which, if we did not enter into, we should miss. Not only should we miss it, but we would not be complete without it.

If we will listen to the heartbeat of each other and humanity, we will hear the great rhythm of the Universe resounding in us.

The friends which our consciousness attracts to us belong to us. Through them the Infinite speaks a Divine language.

God-in-me means that there is One Infinite Person in all people which unites them in the bonds of love and friendship.

The person who loves others and has a feeling of friendship for them will always make friends because the Law of Life is a law of action and reaction.

If we seek friendship we must affirm that God is in us, God is in everyone we shall ever meet, we are already one with all people in God. And then we must accept that because this is true, everyone is one with us in God.

We wish to reap joy, happiness, love, friendship, health, harmony, and success. Could we expect to keep our mind filled with such thoughts for ourself unless it were filled with similar thoughts for others? Of course not. We have a right to expect that what we wish for others will be returned to us through others. We have no right to expect that we can reap where we have not sown.

We must not think of people as better or worse. All people are all right if we meet them in an all-right way. We shall call out of every person whom we meet that which is like our subjective acceptance of Life.

GIVINGNESS

The hand that gives is the hand of God.

It is not in lavish gifts that we find true giving, but in the sweet simplicity of remembrance, in the kindly thought, the tolerant mind, and the gentle act. The one who gives for reward does not give at all; he seeks to bargain, to trade for spiritual gifts, hence he senses a loss in his own giving and finds no completion through the act.

It is only those gifts held in a loose hand that give us any joy; only those gifts scattered to the four winds of heaven can return to us on the eternal circuits of the Divine.

No matter how abundantly the Horn of Plenty may pour out Its universal gifts, there must be a bowl of acceptance, a chalice of expectancy, or the gift cannot be complete. The bowl of acceptance which we hold beneath the outpouring Horn of Plenty is itself a part of the Divine Givingness, for how could there be a givingness unless there were an equal receivingness? It is receivingness which fulfills the givingness and the interaction is only complete when our bowl of acceptance is full.

Compensation is necessary, but there is no way to gain all without first giving all. There is no compromise; the Universe does not bargain with us. It has to be met on Its own terms, but these terms are not arbitrary because God is Love.

Knowing that God is hid in everything, we reveal this Divine Presence to ourselves and to each other in sympathy, in love, in kindness. So we give back into the great and Divine Presence that which It has given to us, knowing that the gift will again be returned, and multiplied.

GOOD AND EVIL

Nothing opposes good, but much seems to contradict it. There is no final power of evil, but the individual builds up a subjective reaction which contradicts his good, denies his wholeness, happiness, and freedom, and builds a barrier between that which he seems to be and that which he feels he ought to be.

If evil were a real entity, then we could not overcome it, but if it is merely one of the patterns of thought which we are weaving, then we may change the pattern. Evil is a negation of good. It will disappear individually and collectively in direct ratio as good dominates the thought.

The knowledge of good overcomes evil, not by fighting it but by nonresisting, nonrecognizing, and refusing to accept it. In the place of the evil the good is known and where it is known it is demonstrated.

We shall have to empty ourselves of everything that does not belong to Good. This does not mean the renunciation of happiness, joy, love, friendship, or accomplishment – only the renunciation of the belief in dualism that settles in our mind like a black cloud of ignorance, fear, and superstition, and becomes the morbidity of our introspection and the hopelessness of our outlook.

Those who are willing to look forward to a greater good, while at the same time carrying into action those constructive precedents which have produced the present good, are the ones who provide a safeguard for true progress.

Every man is ethical who neither lies to himself or others, nor cheats himself or others. Every man is moral who follows whatever the laws of the universe may be. Every man is good who does not think evil.

GUIDANCE

God answers every request at the level of the thought which makes the request. When the scientist listens, the artist imagines, the mathematician calculates, or the poet waits for the muse to guide his fancy into word pictures, all are praying for Divine guidance. Each in his own sphere of action receives as much guidance as he is capable of perceiving.

We may be surrounded by Divine Wisdom, Love, and Intelligence, and still lack Divine guidance. Not that we lack the ability to accept it, for that is the gift of God forever made and forever delivered. But we lack the perception of this guidance and its operation through us.

To feel that a Presence greater than we are is guiding us, is normal; to trust this Presence, is sanity. To desire that the Divine shall express Itself in our mind and project Itself through our thought, is to be receptive to that greater side of our nature that lies open to us in the upper reaches of thought.

There is no doubt but that too much of the vision of the world has failed to reach its goal. It has stranded itself upon the rocks of uncertainty, fear, and unbelief. We need a chart and compass; we need a guide. But not an external one, not someone to tell us what to do or how we ought to do it, not someone who wishes merely to impose his own will on ours. We need an inner guide, and the miracle of it is that we already have this inner guide. It has been there all the time, waiting our acceptance.

We are divinely inspired and intelligently led only insofar as a knowledge greater than we before possessed passes from the invisible atmosphere of the Divine Mind, through our intellect and emotions, into the objective actions of our everyday life.

THE HERE AND NOW

The there and the then, the here and the now, are alike to the Mind that stretches into the past, comprehends the present, and measures the possibilities of the future.

In an attempt to place our finger on the present we find the flow of an invisible Cause already moving the present into the past and introducing a future. Our finger points to one place; the flow knows no place, no time — only Being.

The Infinite has no concept of futurity. It is always *here* and *now* with the creative Mind of God. This is why the desire or prayer must be an already accomplished fact in the mind that conceives it.

The past reveals what we might have done, current events portray our present states of thought, the possibility of the future is already inherent in our imagination.

If we can catch the split second of the eternal now, where the future is no longer bound to the past through a sequence of cause and effect, then today will be free from the thralldom of yesterday and the fear of tomorrow.

The bright and happy tomorrows of which we dream must not be thought of as though the imagination conceived them to be something that is about to take place. Rather, they must become a part of our mental acceptance of the today in which we live.

There is no better time than now. I believe in living while we live and giving while we have — right now, today.

Let your soul sing the song of today, and tomorrow's song will be sweeter.

IMAGINATION

True imagination is not fanciful daydreaming; it is fire from heaven.

We shall never get away from the creative power of our thought. We should use our imagination, will, and emotion to the end that we shall have freedom instead of bondage, joy instead of unhappiness, peace in the place of confusion.

Whenever one makes a demand upon his own creative intelligence or imagination, this demand causes the Law of Mind to do certain things for him. In this way a new creation takes place.

Imagination is one of the gifts bestowed upon man, the thinker. But he has allowed it to become degraded into a curse. He could use it as he was intended to use it — to lift him to the heights.

Our trouble is that we try to drag the Infinite down to finite levels, rather than gradually extending the horizon of our finite levels to take in more and more territory, push the horizon out, and encompass more of the Infinite.

While we continuously remold thought according to the pattern of ancient ideas, we remain bound by previous opinion, bias, and prejudice. We must do something to break down the walls of experience and expand the vision of the soul. Here our imagination comes into play, enabling us to conceive a greater good.

Mind is the only creative Power which science has discovered, and imagination is the chief instrument of Mind, just as feeling is Its principal motivating power.

Life will never pall for the individual who expresses the creative genius of his own soul.

IMMORTALITY

Immortality is not something we bargain with the Almighty for; it is not something that is bought and paid for. It is a gift of heaven. It is the result of the incarnation of God the living Spirit.

Spirit is immortal and eternal, therefore Spirit cannot conceive of death, cessation of action, or the lessening of life.

Let anyone come into contact with real Life and he will experience immortality in the flesh. He will never experience death, he will experience transition.

If the self is not immortal, then we shall never know it, for then death would end all things and there would be nothing left to contemplate this utter oblivion, this complete annihilation. If, on the other hand, death does not end all things and immortality is a fact, then there will never be any lapse in self-knowingness other than the lapse from a sleeping into an awakening state such as we have on this earth.

There is no human *and* Divine, no mortal *and* Immortal. There is, rather, Immortality expressing Itself in time, and Divinity manifesting Itself through the activity of man.

There will never come a time when we will have exhausted the possibilities of infinity, or saturated the possibility of evolution. Because we are dealing with the Infinite, no matter how far we go, we will go farther.

There is an intuition in man that knows he is immortal. Our modern science is proving it, but it is merely verifying by an inductive method something within us that has always known.

There are no finalities in any science, any philosophy, or any religion. Through the continual emergence of the creative Principle any last finality proves to be but the beginning of a new creative series. This eternal spiral, finding its base in the everlasting Reality, will never cease to emerge.

INDIVIDUALITY

There is no real mind or spiritual force outside of or external to the original creative Cause. In no way does this make mere puppets of our individual minds, for our minds are outlets through which the infinite Mind works. Rather than a sense of limitation, this should give us a sense of freedom and a transcendent possibility.

Spirit is the essence of all individuality. With the One Supreme Mind is the possibility of projecting limitless expressions of Itself. Each is unique and different from all others. Thus the Infinite is not divided but multiplied.

We are individuals in a cosmic Wholeness. Each is a unique representation of the one and only Mind and Spirit, and since this

Mind and Spirit is infinite, Its capacity to individualize must likewise be without limit. This is the mystery of unity in multiplicity.

It is important that we recognize the unique presentation of the Infinite in each finite individual, in a way different from Its presentation in any other one, else there would be no variation in Itself and It would be a monotony.

When the individual emerges he is left alone to make all the discoveries for himself, because when he returns to his Father's house he must come back an individualization of the Infinite; he must know himself. Death is not the loss of identity. We are not to be lost in God, but found in God.

You may trust the integrity of your own soul, the continuity of your own life, the eternity and immortality of your own being, with absolute and complete abandonment. It is part of the Divine Nature Itself.

God, or the Father in heaven, is not separated from the Son. The Son is the individualization, the man principle in God, and the God Principle in man.

INTELLIGENCE

There is a creative Intelligence at the center of everything. By the self-recognition of this Intelligence forms and conditions are created. By a shifting around of this self-recognition forms can be made to change their appearance, and their sequence and order, in the visible world. This is the mystery of creation. The inner Principle at work is Spirit.

Intelligence alone is the originating creative Cause. Whether this Intelligence is in what we call man or what we call God, it is the same Intelligence since all intelligence must finally be One.

The intellect is the discerning faculty without which there would be no balance in the individual. We must never belittle intellect.

Without it the Spirit could never come forth into manifestation. It provides the mold through which the intangible becomes the tangible manifestation. All things must start in pure Intelligence and must exist there in essence before they make their appearance in form.

God does not have ends to gain, methods to use, and devious paths to follow to persuade anybody of anything. The Intelligence in the universe presses against everything and when the door is open It comes in. It is already there.

Our individual intelligence has its source in the One Intelligence; however, this does not mean that every act of ours is intelligent. But even the most foolish act of ours would not be possible unless there were an intelligence by which we could commit the foolishness.

The infinite Intelligence must know the answer to every legitimate question. We have immediate access to this Intelligence, and in a very real sense the answer to every question is potential within us because we are within It. We should learn to consciously draw upon It.

JOY

If the great adventure were a closed book, if there were no trails that ran out into the unknown, and if there were no horizons beyond our present experience, the joy would go out of living. But the jubilant soul is a beholding one and the great adventure of life, the great game of living, lies in enthusiastic expectancy of the more yet to come.

We must enter into the joy of Life if we expect the joy of Life to enter into us.

Life has intended us to be glad. There is always a song when we know how to sing it, and always a joy if we can find it.

Life is not meant to be sad, dreary, forlorn, or hopeless. It is not meant to be a funeral dirge. It is meant to be a grand and sublime song of praise, a proclamation of joy, through the acceptance of happiness and wholeness in God.

God is happy, and if we wish to draw happiness into our experience, we must first unify ourselves with the happiness and the joy that God is.

How can we believe in a weeping universe or a sad God or a melancholy First Cause? Such concepts contradict the fundamental necessity of Reality, that God is a synonym for wholeness.

A person filled with joy must lavish it on others; he must share it with them. In this way he multiplies his own happiness.

We should live each day as though it were complete and perfect within itself. We should live each day as though all the joy in the universe were ours now.

LAW

The Universe is eternally just. The Law of Life compels that action and reaction equal each other. Our own act is our judge, nothing else could be, nothing else need be, therefore we are ourselves heaven and hell.

We are the servant of what we obey. The Law serves us and then compels us to serve It. It is at once love and hate, freedom and bondage, because of Itself It is One Law ready to create any form.

God does not punish the mathematician who fails to find the right answer to his problem. This unsolved problem punishes him until he secures the desired result. Thus sin and punishment, righteousness and salvation, are but logical reactions of a universe of Law to the life of the individual.

If we are dealing with a Power which actually makes things out of Itself by Itself becoming, or taking the form of, the thing that It makes, and if this Power is Spirit, then we can easily see that the Word of God is also the Law of God. The Word of God is a conscious act, and the Law of God is a mechanical reaction.

Because the Law reflects the exact images of thought we think into It, and has no other choice in the matter, then it follows that no matter what the Law now may be maintaining as being true about us, through a new process of thinking we may so completely change Its action as to alter the experience.

One cannot use the creative Law of Mind most effectively without using It consistently and persistently and very simply, accepting, as every scientific mind must accept, the fact that principles do not change or alter their courses to suit our convenience. We are subject to them; they are not subject to us.

LIFE

There is no one who can explain what Life is, or why Life is, because what Life is is evidenced by what It does.

Life is a gift, we did not earn it. Humanly speaking, we are not good enough to have made it or bad enough to destroy it.

That within us which enables us to be aware is the Spirit that is incarnated in us. It ever reaches out and up into higher levels bringing more and more awareness to the point of our consciousness.

Our whole process is the demonstrating of a greater peace, a greater joy, a greater spontaneity, and a fuller, happier, more successful and more vital life. Ours is a mission of entering more completely into life for the joy of living.

We must enter into the spirit of living if we wish to really live and to drink deeply from that fountain of Life which wells up from within.

The happiness of the individual life is essential to the universal Wholeness, for thus does It find an extension of Itself.

There is no successful life without a complete conviction of the eternality of one's own consciousness. The Essence of Life is ever-present. It is the intellect which molds this Essence into form. The Essence is already here and conviction measures It out.

Life is a blackboard before which we stand and write the words which govern us. We hold both chalk and eraser in our hands. The blackboard allows us to use either, according to our power of choice. If we have made incorrect marks upon the blackboard, we need not condemn ourselves, nor need we go through life bemoaning their presence. We may erase them, but the hand that holds the eraser must do the erasing.

LOVE

Love is the great Reality; hate the great negation.

Perfect love casts out fear. As the sun dissolves darkness, so love conquers hate. We are not to flee from the wrath to come, but to perceive the love that *is*.

Love is a self-surrender which, instead of depriving, fulfills. Thus it is written that love is the fulfillment of the law.

Love will find the solution within itself to every problem, will answer every question. It is the lodestone of Life, the center of Reality, the heart of the Universe, and it will ultimately win and vanquish every foe.

Hate destroys until love heals, for love is greater than hate and finally love is triumphant and all the misunderstandings of hate are consumed in its Divine passion, its Universal flame.

Love is the victor in every case. Love breaks down the iron bars of thought, shatters the walls of false belief, severs the chains of bondage which thought has imposed, and sets the captive free.

If one makes himself receptive to the idea of love, he becomes lovable. To the degree that he embodies love, he is love, so people who love are loved.

Divine Love interprets Itself to everyone who knows love, comes to everyone who senses love, impersonates Itself in forms which are human, in experiences which are Divine.

The only man who knows anything about love is the man who loves.

Every act of human affection and love, of generous giving and receiving, of kindly relations with others, is an extension of the Spirit of Life flowing through us. Life is the great Giver and each one of us is a distributor.

MAN

Man himself is some part of the eternal mystery which he seeks to solve.

Man is the inevitable necessity of God's Self-expression.

The overdwelling Presence, which is God, is the indwelling person, which is man. And there can be no separation whatsoever. God in man, as man, is man.

We deal with the real man only when we deal with the whole man. We deal with the whole man only when we deal with the spiritual, mental, and physical faculties working in unity.

The only thing we know anything about that has self-consciousness is man. Man is the highest development of the evolutionary process on this planet, hence must be the most nearly like his Source — the most Godlike. And since the higher form of intelligence must govern all lower forms, by reason of the fact that all forms are a result of one infinite Mind operating at different levels, then man must have control over his environment as soon as he comes to understand the nature of himself and his environment.

When God produced an instrument — man — through which God could consciously act, the advent of choice and will enabled man to accomplish that which nature had not done specifically.

Back of the known is the Unknown. The Unknown Man is the real man. The known man is simply as much of a revelation of the Unknown as the intellect conceives at the present place in its evolution.

In the Divine Mind man must already be, in principle, the sum total of whatever he is evolving into. To hold to this Divine Sonship as a present reality is one of the first steps toward the goal of human endeavor.

MIND

We are all rooted in one common soil. This common soil is the Soul of the Universe, the Mind of God. The mind of man is the Mind of God in man, and as such partakes of the same original creativeness as the Mind of God.

There is no boundary line around the mind of man, for the mind of man is, in its last analysis, the Mind of God.

Everything is in Mind; nothing moves but Mind. Intelligence is back of everything, acting through a Law of Mind which is specific, definite, and real.

Just as the engine is not the engineer, so even the Law of Mind is not the Mind using the Law; there is a user. And if the user uses the Law destructively, It will temporarily set destructive things in motion and they will not work out well. Finally that which is constructive must prevail.

By intuition we know God. It is the Mind of God recognizing Itself which constitutes this intuitional perception.

The alleged mediators between God and man are theological misconceptions. The mind itself is the sole and only medium.

Mind is a fluent force. It is forever taking form and forever deserting the form which It has taken.

Since Mind is the only actor, cause, and power that there is, then the measure of our thought must certainly be the measure of our accomplishment. If we want a sure index of the measure of our thoughts, we can get it accurately by seeing what we are bringing into our outer life.

There is possible to the mind a state of awareness which rises above all confusion, apprehension, fear, or doubt, and looking over such conditions can dissipate them by the Divinity of its own Godlike glance.

PEACE

The peaceful mind is calm in the midst of confusion, but the mind distraught by the events of the day, fearful of the future, morbidly introspecting the past in its imagination, finds no repose and is continuously tormented by itself.

Peace is brought about through a conscious unity of the personal man with the inner Principle of his life, that underlying current flowing from a Divine center, pressing ever outward into expression.

The moment of transition from external confusion to inward peace is indicated as we pass through the negation of opposites to the affirmation of unity.

A change in affairs does not necessarily bring peace. Friends cannot make the gift, money cannot purchase it. Nothing can bring peace but the revelation of the individual to himself.

Such peace as any man possesses comes from a conscious or unconscious agreement with the Universe, a noncombativeness toward It.

The Divine does not come to us bringing an olive branch of peace with which to allay our confusion. The Divine knows no confusion. It persists in remaining true to Its own nature. The nature of God *is* peace.

We say that God is peace, but the only God of peace we know about is the peace we have in ourselves which reveals, not a God *of* peace, but a God who *is* peace. God does not acquire qualities. God is the Essence; the quality is merely the way It manifests Itself.

The Spirit is ever calm and filled with peace for It has no enemies to contend with or against.

The real Fatherhood of God and the true brotherhood of man must be understood before the world can live in peace.

PERSONALITY

Human personality is not to be scoffed at as though it were an illusion. It is not an illusion, but the grandest conclusion God has yet drawn in our understanding of Himself.

Personality is an objective evidence of that Divine inner spiritual individuality that can never be divorced from the final Reality which is God. Each is already possessed of a personality which no person can reproduce.

It is impossible to avoid the conclusion that a universal Personalness pervades all creation and is back of all motion. But this universal Personalness rises through man into personality. Indeed it *is* his personality.

The Infinite both is and is not a person. Not a person in the sense of a huge human being or an infinite human being, but a person in the sense of a self-knowing conscious intelligence, with volition and power to express. From the infinite Self-knowingness of Spirit arises our power to know. From the universal Mind our minds spring. The Infinite multiplies Itself through the finite, and finds innumerable avenues of expression through personalities.

We can accept the whole theory of evolution and still believe in an intelligent Purposiveness working through evolution. This intelligent Purposiveness not only projects Itself in what we call "nature," but Its aim is to produce what we call "personality."

The universal Spirit is at the root of all personality. It is the unexpressed wholeness of the real self and as such holds within Itself the Divine Ideal of what we are and what we are evolving into. Consciously to cooperate with It is consciously to take part in the furtherance of our evolution.

It is an inevitable axiomatic necessity that even that which is Universal must be intimately personal to that which It personalizes.

There is no myself that hinders what I am outside of what I think myself to be.

POWER

It is not through human determination, but by the silent workings of the Spirit through our organized thought that the Divine imparts of Its Power to man. We are chemists in the laboratory of the Infinite; what shall we produce?

Whatever the ultimate Power of the universe is, It is One; and since It is One It is undivided, therefore It is here. Since It is here, It is where we are and what we are within ourselves, and only within ourselves shall we discover God.

Because of Its indivisibility, unity, and omnipresence, every bit of the Intelligence of the Universe and every atom of the Power of the Law of the Universe, backs every word we speak, whatever its objectification might be, because the Universe knows nothing about big or little, important or unimportant.

If we are dealing with limitless Power, then It can bring things to pass for us which we could have no possible way of knowing how to accomplish for ourselves. It touches all points at all times and knows every means necessary to any particular end. We choose but we need not outline.

Before final deliverance can be made we must conform to the nature of harmony, truth, and unity, else we should find ourselves equipped with all Power, and not knowing how to rightly use It, we could destroy ourselves. We can well ponder long and earnestly on the thought that the Universe is really foolproof. Real power is delivered only when we are spiritually ready for it.

Power unused will do nothing. We must recognize spiritual Power, and then use It.

The power of our word is in the conviction that it has power.

It is not what we believe that makes truth; but we are fortunate if what we believe is truth, for then all the Power of heaven and earth is allied with us.

PRAYER

Let us convert prayer into a conscious communion with the Invisible, and faith into the dynamic use of spiritual Power. Let us take the "mist" out of the mysteries. Let us understand that one Divine Power has always existed and has always interpreted Itself to men by interpreting Itself through them.

It is a self-evident fact that any natural power must express itself in terms of the channel or instrument through which it flows. This must also be true of prayer. The prayer which merely asks for something without, at the same time, providing a mental equivalent of the need for which it asks, automatically makes it impossible for the gift to be made.

Affirmative in its acceptance, and seeking to become an embodiment of the essence of its own realization, prayer will yet be discovered to be the most dynamic force in the lives of individuals and in the destinies of peoples.

A man should not desire to spend his entire time praying, but should seek to make his work a prayer, his life a song, his living an art, his believing an act.

Prayer is an inward and not an outward movement, and since consciousness cannot separate itself from itself, nor mind conceive anything unrelated to itself, and since thought is always an inner movement, it follows that prayer is a movement of consciousness upon itself. The prayer of faith, then, is a movement of consciousness which accepts its own affirmation.

Prayer contradicts no scientific fact, affirms no impossible state of being, contradicts no law of nature, but rises gently to the comprehension of the Divine Presence as an agency of good, of right action, and of immediate availability.

If we would pray and prosper we must believe that the Spirit is both willing and able to make the gift. But since the Spirit can only give us what we take, and since the taking is a mental act, we must train the mind to believe and to accept. This is the secret of the power of prayer.

REALITY

The spiritual world of Reality is not afar off. Indeed, it is now here, but we fail to see it. It matters not what we call this Reality. All have invoked Its power, each in his own way. The unknown God has been proclaimed by all races and the breath of the Invisible has sent healing to all who have believed in It. The refreshing winds of heaven blow alike to each and to all. It is the Spirit that quickeneth.

Reality is not something we shall finally attain, but something which we now experience, though we are largely ignorant of it.

There is no mediator between ourselves and the eternal Reality. There is no mediator between God and man but the Spirit in man.

That is, we approach Reality through the self, for the self is the indwelling Spirit of God incarnate in the human.

When thought knows, understands, and embodies Reality, it becomes and is Reality, and Reality is Power.

Anything that emanates from the eternal changeless Reality will have to be of like nature with It because it is of It and cannot contradict It. If it did, that slight movement out of variance with the whole would destroy the whole.

The illusion is not in the thing, but in the way we look at it. The illusion is our projection against the face of Reality. The face of Reality has never changed.

Where is the darkness when the light enters? Where is the lie when the truth is told? It is as though it never were. It was only a supposition. The world has yet to understand that there is a great difference between a false belief and Reality, and that whenever Reality enters, the false belief tends to sink into its native nothingness.

REBIRTH

Let us let the dead self bury the dead self, and let new hope rise on the horizon of our experience as the realization comes to each that all the long yesterdays we have experienced are tales which are told, ships that have passed in the night.

Today the horizon is clear, the voyage starts anew, we are reborn. The true resurrection is not only from this life into the next; it takes place daily and hourly as we shed the limited concepts of life and come into the vineyard to gather the fruit of the Spirit hanging rich from the vines of God.

A person may be reborn, remade, and renewed in mind and body just through taking a little time to get acquainted with his better self, just through coming to recognize the invisible and almost unknown guest who accompanies everyone through life — the spiritual Presence within.

We are all on the pathway of an eternal existence, born anew daily, born of the Divine Spirit, growing into the knowledge of what it really means to be a Son of God. And gradually as this knowledge comes to us and we follow the Divine leading, we shall grow in spiritual power.

We should resurrect ourselves to the joy and simplicity and spontaneity of Life and leave the corpses of our dead yesterdays in the tomb of their own obscurity. We should live more abundantly in God this day. When we shall come out of our tomb of ignorance and disbelief, how glorious shall be the dawn!

In our own thought, with silent trust, faith, and childlike acceptance, we may, if we will, uproot all of the old patterns that have limited us, and in their place replant a new Eden in which we may live in happiness, joy, and peace. And is it not wonderful that we, and only we, shall choose; and we, only we, shall execute! And is it not wonderful to know that we have this privilege now, today!

SELF-RECOGNITION

The concept of a Divine Presence which is personal to him is the basis of every man's reaction to life. No matter who he is or where he comes from, what he does or what he believes, fundamentally at the root of all his concepts of life is his conscious or unconscious recognition of his relationship to the Universe in which he lives.

Spirit is that inner Essence and Intelligence at the center of all things which by self-recognition becomes the person, place, or form recognized. By a shifting around of this self-recognition forms can be made to change their appearance and their sequence and order in the visible world.

Self-recognition is the keystone to the arch of perfection. To divorce God from his Universe, including man, is not only a grave mistake, it is impossible.

When we learn to make inner self-recognition the starting point of our lives, we shall have caught the secret of the ages. For this is the way that Spirit creates. The first and most necessary recognition is that of our relationship to the Spirit Itself. This is the most essential recognition and all others flow from it. We must learn to see the Spirit in everyone and in everything.

The only thing standing between the essence and atmosphere of the Spirit and Its personification through man, and in creation, is recognition. The fruits of right belief have always fallen from the tree of faith.

As we come to a recognition of what and who we are, we will see that we do not have to contend with anything on earth. We do not have to struggle to find a place for ourselves in the universe. In the sight of the Spirit, which is also in the sight of our own spiritual natures, we are part of Its expression, no matter where we are.

SPIRIT

Spirit emerges through all. It embraces all ages, encompasses all periods, is present at all times. Uncreated, It creates; unformed, It gives form; unborn, It gives birth.

The standards of the race are always in a state of flux, changing from generation to generation, from day to day, and from individual to individual. But the standard of Spirit is ageless, changeless, unvarying. It is perfection, nothing less. When the level of the individual's thinking is divorced from that of the world and raised to that of the Spirit, his standard changes from that of imperfection to perfection. And this is the true norm.

Men will come and men will go, friend and foe alike may fall away, but always the soul shall be thrown back upon itself. The indwelling Spirit that lives in the secret place of our lives will ever be with us.

The objective world is the fruitage of Spirit. Spirit and matter are two ends of the same thing.

Running through the impermanent, through the changing, the fluctuating, the moving, there is something that never moves. This is what we mean by the Spirit.

Spirit is never manifest through us except on the terms of Its own nature. It will not be finite; It will not be less than perfect.

The one who seeks to prove the supremacy of spiritual thought over apparent material resistance must know that the Spirit has no opposition and knows none.

The approach to Spirit should be direct, and there should be an acceptance in the mind that there will be a direct response. The Spirit is everywhere present; there is no more or less of It in one place than in another. There is no place where God is not.

SUCCESS

If we are to succeed, we must think success. If we are to be happy, we must think happily. If we are to be well, we must think healthful, constructive thoughts. If we are to get over confusion, we must think peace. The mind cannot accept what it rejects.

It is the ability to think affirmatively that gives us the consciousness and the power to lift an experience out of chaos, out of lack and limitation, into happiness and abundance.

We are neither forgotten men nor are we favorites of God. The question of success and failure remains where it belongs, in the mastery of ignorance, in the overcoming of superstition, fear, and doubt, in the elimination of destructive methods, and in the conscious reversal of thought processes which deny the eternal Good.

Work without vision is drudgery, but vision without work is self-deception. The well-balanced man can walk with his head in the clouds and still keep his feet solidly planted on the ground. Faith and work are ineffective when separated.

Each in his own particular way is fulfilling the purpose of the Life that is within him. We have every right to expect that our contribution will in turn draw to us ample supply, high success, and an ever-increasing expression of good. Only one person in the entire universe can hinder an individual from accomplishing this, and that person is himself.

It is wrong to be unsuccessful, but success also means more than dollars and cents. Success means mental growth and spiritual attainment. As the greater includes the lesser, so mental and spiritual growth includes material success, bringing with it personal happiness and temporal satisfaction.

There is no real success without happiness, no happiness without peace, no peace without spiritual security.

TREATMENT

A spiritual mind treatment — an effective prayer — is a statement acted on by Law, embodying the concrete idea of our desires, and accompanied by an unqualified faith that the Law works for us as we work with It.

Spiritual mind treatment is always based on the proposition that man's being is rooted in pure Spirit. It is always for the purpose of indrawing Spirit, never for the purpose of influencing another. Spiritual realization is a dynamic sense of the presence, the power, and the availability of good, and whatever thought of limitation or image of obstruction intrudes upon this recognition of Truth must be resolutely set aside.

There is in a spiritual mind treatment just exactly as much and no more than we put into it. The treatment is the nucleus, the seed, the idea around which the energies of Spirit play. Just as the creative forces of the soil, sun, and air take a seed and produce a plant, so spiritual mind treatment is a concept through which universal Law flows, producing a form like the idea given It.

We understand that mind in essence and mind in form are one and the same thing. We are not spiritualizing matter to heal disease, nor materializing Spirit to control matter. There is no such thing as a spiritual control of a material universe, as though Spirit were separate from it, for such a theory involves suppositional opposites and would annihilate fundamental unity.

The practice of spiritual mind treatment is not so much something we do as it is something we know. The doing is a mental process; the knowing is a state of consciousness.

It is impossible to divorce spiritual realization from true spiritual mind treatment. It would be like trying to take the heat out of fire and still have it hot, or the wetness out of water and still have it wet.

UNITY

From the One outcrops the many without ever destroying the unity of the One. Each one of us has all of God to himself without taking away from the all of God that every other one has.

Underlying all forms is an essential Unity that is everywhere and responds to us at all times, whether we know it or not. But It can respond to us only through our mental images. When we think of It as limitless, then It becomes expanded, so to speak, in our experience.

What we must do is to so recognize our unity with Life that It increasingly finds expression through us; then whatever good thing we desire, this thing will become a part of our experience.

When we consider that all creation, ourselves included, is a projection of the originating Spirit which of necessity must work from the basis of Its own Unity, then we shall see that a Power and Intelligence which is Infinite could not project opposing forces without destroying both Itself and Its projection. There is a common root to all things, people, and events.

The Mind of God and the mind of man are one and the same. The difference is in degree and not in essence. The whole Universe is undivided and indivisible; all of It must exist at any and every point within It. Center and circumference are identical.

If a man believes in purgatory and the devil and all the superstitions that have been shoved down people's emotional throats, he will always be sick, unhappy, insecure, always have a sense of guilt and anxiety. There has to come a clearance at the very root of the matter where the person can come to see there is nothing between God and himself..

WHOLENESS

The Universe is a spiritual system, a Divine order, a unitary, everlasting, and indestructible wholeness, so near, so close to us, that thought carries with it the weight of its own creation.

The Spirit in Its original state must be ever-present with us, It refuses to be divided. Consquently, the eternal Wholeness Itself is immediately at the point of our perception – all of It.

All is One. We are not turning, then, from the human to the Divine, but the Divine is turning to Itself, giving expression to Itself. The self comes bearing its own gifts.

There could not be a universal Wholeness which is the cause of all that is without Itself becoming the effect of that of which

It is the cause. Therefore, the cause and the effect transpire in the same medium and are but two ends of a polarity of an action and a reaction in a unitary field.

The Spirit cannot manifest chaotically because It is a Cosmos; It cannot manifest dualistically because It is a unitary Wholeness; It cannot manifest on any plane without reproducing on that plane what is true about It on every plane, because It is Universal.

The higher self must subdue the lower. This is the true victory. This is the end of the cycle of necessity and the emancipation of the soul from the thralldom of its material sense. It is really a salvation from a part to the Whole.

There is no isolated good, no separated good, no absolutely individual good. This does not mean that it is impossible to individualize good, but that the individual mind is already a part of the universal Wholeness, which truth, when discovered and embodied, leads to its proper manifestation — the wholeness of the individualized life.